Basketball Rules
IN PICTURES

Edited by A. G. Jacobs

Consultant: Stewart C. Paxton

EXECUTIVE DIRECTOR, INTERNATIONAL ASSOCIATION
OF APPROVED BASKETBALL OFFICIALS, INC.

Illustrated by George Kraynak

GROSSET & DUNLAP   PUBLISHERS   NEW YORK

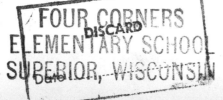

FOUR CORNERS
DISCARD
ELEMENTARY SCHOOL
SUPERIOR, WISCONSIN

COPYRIGHT ©1966 BY A. G. JACOBS

ALL RIGHTS RESERVED.

PUBLISHED SIMULTANEOUSLY IN CANADA.

LIBRARY OF CONGRESS CATALOG CARD NUMBER: 63-12937

*Dedicated to
the hard-working officials — too
often more blamed than praised*

Basketball Rules, Officiating, and Techniques, a set of six color film strips on which this book is based, is available from the School Film Service, 549 W. 123rd Street, Suite 12 E New York, New York 10027

PRINTED IN THE UNITED STATES OF AMERICA

INTRODUCTION

The game of basketball was invented in 1891 by Dr. James A. Naismith, an instructor at the International Young Men's Christian Association Training School (now Springfield College) in Springfield, Massachusetts. He did so at the suggestion of Dr. Luther H. Gulick, head of the YMCA physical training staff, who had become concerned over the drop in the club's attendance during the winter months. The cause, he reasoned, was that there was no competitive winter athletic program, the chief means by which the YMCA recruited its members. The problem of creating an indoor team game to compete with the outdoor varieties was turned over to Dr. Naismith.

Dr. Naismith studied the existing outdoor team games and came to several conclusions. First, most team games used a ball which was either hit or driven toward a goal; but if a ball were used indoors, it would have to be light and large, for safety and control. Second, most outdoor team sports emphasized roughness and physical contact, which would be highly dangerous indoors, so running with the ball and physical contact were eliminated. Third, the roughest play in outdoor sports occurred when both teams congregated near a goal; this possible danger was eliminated by placing the goal above the heads of the contestants. Dr. Naismith used two empty peach baskets as goals, threw in a soccer ball, and basketball was born.

The inventor established 13 basic rules, which were written out and posted on the bulletin board for all to see. These rules remained the basic rules of the game for the next fifty years.

The simplicity, logic, and adaptability of basketball gave impetus to its acceptance and popularity, and by 1913 the rules were printed in 30 languages and there were an estimated 20,000,000 players throughout the world.

Today basketball is one of the most popular sports in the world, and it is safe to say that almost every man, woman, and child in the United States under fifty years of age has played it at one time or another and is at least vaguely familiar with its rules. Television has increased its popularity as a spectator sport, and its designation as an Olympic event has given it status as one of the world's great sports. The International Association of Approved Basketball Officials is an organization which is filling a worldwide need of clarifying and interpreting the application of the rules of the game.

This book, in its small way, is intended to help the beginner understand the game of basketball as it is played today. It is by no means complete, and each player, spectator, or television viewer is advised to read the rules printed in the back of the book.

210

Throughout the book we have used the letter U to denote the Umpire, and R to denote the Referee; the Lead Official is indicated by the letter L and the Trail Official by the letter T. In the drawings, the team with the white jerseys is the offensive team.

The editor wishes to express sincere appreciation to Mr. Bruce Bassett, the popular player from Northwestern University, for his help with the floor plays, and especially to Mr. Stewart C. Paxton, Executive Director of IAABO, for his ever-available help in making this book possible.

A. G. JACOBS

CONTENTS

BASKETBALL

Basketball is a game played by two teams of five players each. The purpose of each team is to score by throwing the ball through its own basket and to prevent the opposing team from scoring.

THE BASKETBALL COURT

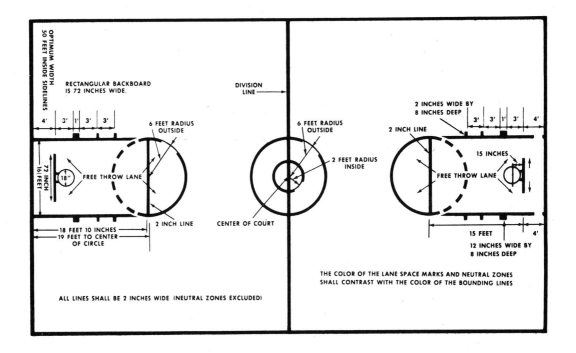

COURT DIMENSIONS

HIGH SCHOOL: 50 feet wide by 84 feet long.
COLLEGE: 50 feet wide by 94 feet long.

The playing court should be clearly marked with sidelines and end lines. There shall be at least 3 feet of unobstructed space outside the lines.

THE BALL

The ball is spherical in shape and should be an approved shade of orange or natural tan in color. The weight must not be less than 20 ounces or more than 22 ounces.

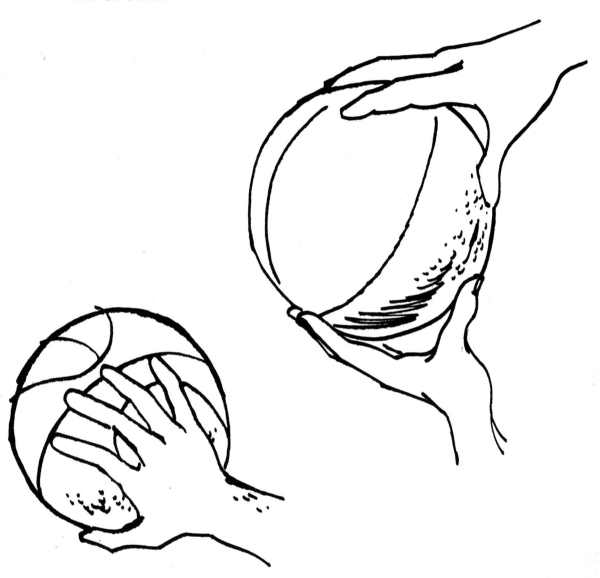

CIRCUMFERENCE OF THE BALL

BELOW SENIOR HIGH SCHOOLS: a minimum of 29 inches and a maximum of 29½ inches.

ADULTS: a minimum of 29½ inches and a maximum of 30 inches.

The home team provides the ball, which must meet the specifications of the rules.

THE BASKETS

The metal ring is 18 inches in diameter. Each basket has 12 attachment loops. The basket is so constructed that the ball is checked momentarily as it passes through the hoop. The ring is securely attached to the backboard. The upper edge of the rim is 10 feet above and parallel to the floor, and is equidistant from the vertical edges of the backboard.

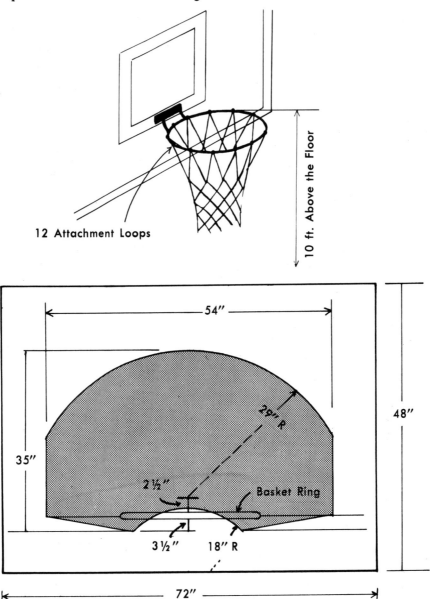

THE BACKBOARDS

The material used for the backboards should be rigid, flat, and either white or transparent. The dimensions are:

RECTANGULAR BACKBOARD: 4 feet vertically by 6 feet horizontally.
FAN-SHAPED BACKBOARD: 54 inches wide at the widest point.

8

BEFORE THE GAME

The officials bring the opposing captains to the center of the floor for introductions. The Referee is responsible for bringing the visiting captain and the Umpire brings the captain of the home team. After introductions the Referee explains ground rules and indicates the color each team will be called (the color of the team's jersey). The Referee indicates the choice of baskets to the spectators.

To start the game the Referee tosses the ball in the air at the center of the court. It is the Referee's duty to see that the toss is straight and that the ball is not tapped until it reaches its full height. After the toss the Referee stands in place and allows all of the ten players to go ahead of him. He then assumes the position of the Trail Official. The Umpire leads the play after the jump ball and is called the Lead Official.

LENGTH OF GAME

Professional	two halves of 24 minutes each (12-minute quarters)	30 minutes rest between halves 2 minutes rest between quarters
College	two halves of 20 minutes each (10-minute quarters)	15 minutes rest between halves
High School	two halves of 16 minutes each (8-minute quarters)	10 minutes rest betweeen halves 1 minute rest between quarters
Young players	two halves of 12 minutes each (6-minute quarters)	10 minutes rest between halves 1 minute rest between quarters

There are many ways of moving the ball down the floor. The best method of insuring accuracy is to control the ball with the tips of the fingers. This holds true for throwing, batting, receiving, shooting, dribbling, etc.

A player may choose to use one of many passes — depending on his ability and the play situation. He may choose to use a one- or two-handed bounce pass, a backward bounce pass, a one- or two-handed push pass, a chest pass, or a pass of his own creation.

THE ONE-HANDED PASS

This pass is not too accurate but is useful in getting the ball down the length of the court.

11

FOUR CORNERS
ELEMENTARY SCHOOL
SUPERIOR, WISCONSIN

17249.

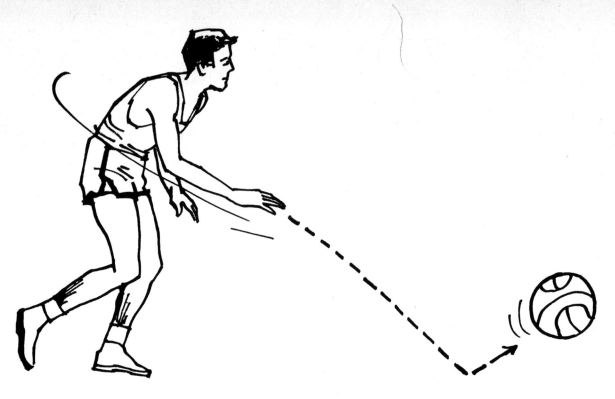

THE BOUNCE PASS

The bounce pass is used most often in pivot plays.

THE TWO-HANDED CHEST PASS

This is the most accurate of the various passes. The step forward on the two-handed chest pass helps produce a good follow through.

HANDING THE BALL

A player may hand the ball to a teammate.

THE DRIBBLE

The dribble is ball movement by a player who throws or taps the ball in the air or onto the floor and then touches it once or several times or catches it.

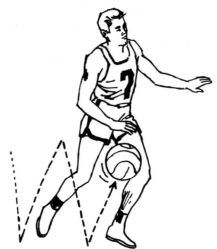

A player sometimes uses a high bounce in the dribble for speed when he is primarily interested in getting the ball down the court.

The same player might use a low bounce in the dribble for more accuracy or when in a relatively tight situation, such as when trying to get around his opponent or when trying to knife in toward the basket for a lay-up shot.

The dribble ends when the player permits the ball to come to rest while he is in possession of it, or when he loses control of the ball, or when he touches the ball with both hands at once.

14

FLOOR POSITION

A player is entitled to a normal floor position not occupied by an opponent, provided he does not cause personal contact by taking such a position.

THE SCREEN PASS

A player may use a screen, which is a legal action of having another player, without causing contact, delay or prevent an opponent from reaching a desired position.

SHOOTING

Shots for the basket may be made from anywhere on the court. A player may choose from a variety of shots the one best suited to the game situation or to his special abilities.

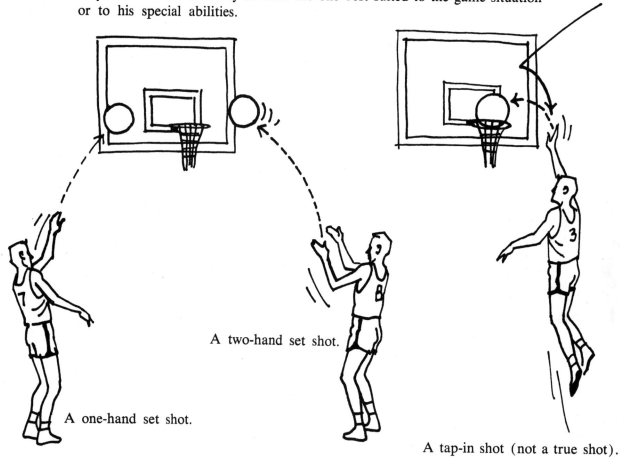

A two-hand set shot.

A one-hand set shot.

A tap-in shot (not a true shot).

16

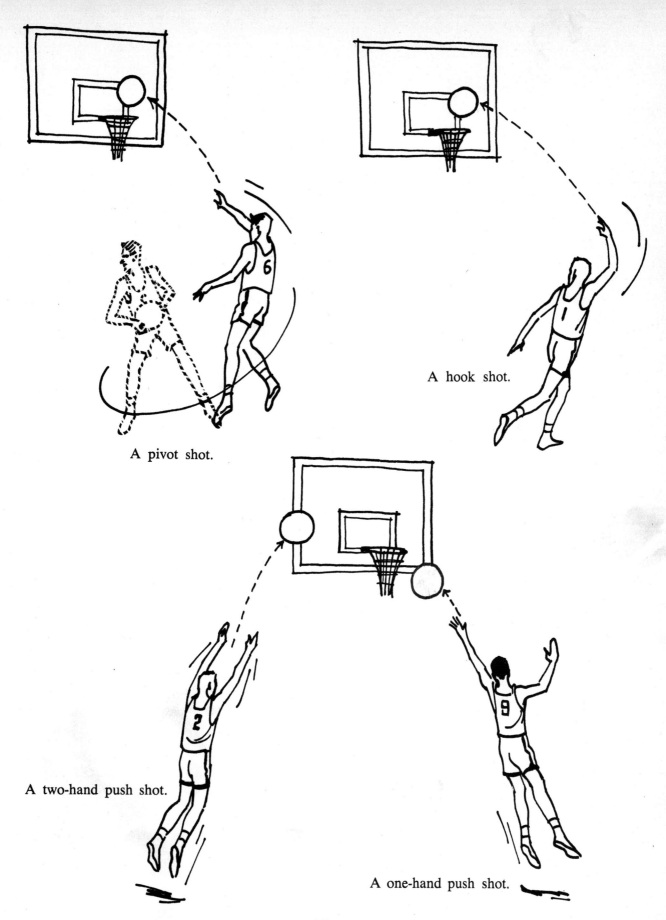

A pivot shot.

A hook shot.

A two-hand push shot.

A one-hand push shot.

SCORING

A goal is made when a live ball enters the basket from above and remains in the basket or passes through it. Each field goal counts 2 points. A goal from a free throw counts 1 point.

The winning team is the one which has the greater number of points when the game ends.

EXTRA PERIODS

If the score is tied at the end of the second half, play shall continue without change of baskets for one or more extra periods with a one-minute intermission before each extra period.

For games played in halves, the length of each extra period shall be 5 minutes. In games played in quarters, the length of each extra period shall be 3 minutes. As many such periods as are necessary to break the tie shall be played.

The game ends if at the end of any extra period the score is not tied.

SUBSTITUTIONS

A substitute reports to the scorer, giving his name and number. He may enter the game only after the scorer sounds his horn and he is beckoned into the court by the official.

GAME PROCEDURE

A player must get the ball out of his team's back court and over the center line within 10 seconds of gaining possession. The Trail Official is responsible for the calling of a violation of the 10-second rule. If there is a violation, the Trail Official will signify same to the scorekeepers by holding both hands up high, showing 10 fingers.

Note how the Lead Official has moved down court in anticipation of the play there.

HELD BALL

A held ball occurs when two opponents have one or both hands so firmly on the ball that neither can gain possession without undue roughness.

The Trail Official is responsible for calling a held ball in the front court when a closely guarded player holds the ball and is unable to pass or deliberately withholds the ball from play. (A player in control of the ball is closely guarded when his opponent is in guarding stance at a distance not exceeding 6 feet.)

JUMP BALL

The ball is put in play in the *center* restraining circle with a jump between two opponents at the beginning of each quarter and extra period, after a double foul, or after the last free throw following a false double foul.

After a held ball, the official puts the ball in play with a jump in the center of the *nearest* restraining circle. The jump begins when the ball leaves the official's hands. The jump ends when the tapped ball touches one of the eight non-jumpers, the floor, the basket, or the backboard.

At other times the ball is put in play by a jump ball at the center of the restraining circle which is *nearest* the spot where the ball goes out-of-bounds, a double free throw violation occurs, the ball lodges in a basket support, or the ball becomes dead when neither team is in control and no goal, infraction, or end of period is involved.

FREE THROW

A free throw is a privilege given a player to score one point by an unhindered throw for goal from within the free throw line circle and behind the free throw line. It starts when the ball is given to the player at the free throw line, or is placed on the line. The ball is alive when placed at the player's disposal. A free throw ends when the ball touches the ring or backboard, or when a goal has been scored.

A free throw is unsuccessful when it does not enter the hoop from above, hits the backboard without touching the rim, or falls short without either touching the rim or the backboard.

If a player is awarded two free throws, it is the responsibility of the Lead Official to secure the ball and return it to the Trail Official who will again put the ball at the disposal of the free thrower.

When the free throw is unsuccessful, the ball is given to the opposing team at the spot where the free throw line, if extended, would intersect the sideline.

VIOLATIONS

A violation is a rule infraction.

An example of a violation is touching the boundary line on a throw-in.

A player commits a violation by:

Carrying the ball into the court on a throw-in.

Touching the ball in the court before it has been touched by another player after a throw-in.

Having any part of the body over the boundary line before the ball has been passed across the line.

Becoming the thrower-in after an official has designated another player.

Causing the ball to go out of bounds.

Touching the boundary line on a throw-in.

Reaching through the plane of the boundary line on a throw-in. (Allowances should be made if space is limited.)

Running with the ball.

Intentionally kicking the ball. (An unintentional brush by the ball is not considered a violation.)

Dribbling a second time after the first dribble has ended. (Exception: When a player has lost control of the ball because of a try for goal, a bat by an opponent, or a pass or a fumble which has been touched by another player.)

Striking the ball with the fist.

Causing the ball to pass through the basket from below.

Making more than one air dribble while dribbling.

Swinging arms or elbows excessively, even though there is no contact with an opponent.

Controlling the ball in the back court for more than 10 consecutive seconds.

Touching the ball or basket when the ball is on or within either basket.

Touching the ball on its downward flight over the basket while the entire ball is above the basket ring level. If the violation is at the opponent's basket, the offended team is awarded one point on a free throw and two points in any other case.

It is *not* a violation if the player has his hand legally in contact with the ball and the contact continues after the ball enters the hoop; he may or may not touch the basket.

Remaining for more than 3 seconds in the free throw lane while the ball is in control of the player's team.

PENALTY FOR VIOLATIONS

The penalty for a violation is a throw-in by the opponents.

The ball becomes dead or remains dead when a violation occurs. The ball is awarded to a nearby opponent for a throw-in at the out-of-bounds spot nearest the violation.

If the ball passes through a basket during a dead ball period immediately following a violation, no point is scored.

The ball is awarded to an opponent out-of-bounds at either end of the free throw line extended of the goal through which the ball was thrown.

The ball is handed to an opponent out-of-bounds after all violations and player control fouls. The Trail Official handles all balls on his side and end line. He hands the ball to the player. He does not toss it. The Trail Official stands between the player and the basket being attacked.

FREE THROW VIOLATIONS

A player commits a free throw violation by:

Stepping over the free throw line while making a free throw.

Stepping over (or on) the lane boundary. (Applies to player on either team.)

Taking more than 10 seconds to make a free throw after the ball has been placed at disposal of player.

Disconcerting the player attempting the free throw.

Occupying a wrong space adjacent to the end line during a try for goal on a free throw. (Opponents of the free thrower must occupy alternate lane spaces adjacent to the end line during the try.)

After a free throw violation the ball is put in play as follows:

If the violation is by the free thrower or his teammate, no point can be scored on that throw. The ball becomes dead when the violation occurs and is put in play by any opponent who may take the ball for a throw-in to either side of the court where the free throw line extended intersects the sideline.

When the violation is by the opponent of the free thrower, and the free throw is *unsuccessful,* the ball is put in play by a substitute free throw attempted by the same free-thrower.

When the violation is by the opponent of the free thrower, and the free throw is *successful,* the violation is disregarded and the goal counts. The ball is put in play again by awarding it to the opponents for a throw-in at the end line.

The Trail Official is responsible for observing violations along the far free throw lane.

PERSONAL FOUL

A personal foul is a player foul which involves contact with an opponent while the ball is alive or after the ball is in possession of a player for a throw-in.

A player commits a personal foul by:

Holding an opponent.

Pushing an opponent.

Charging into an opponent.

Tripping an opponent.

Impeding the progress of an opponent by using the body in other than a normal position.

Making contact with ball holder from behind — a form of pushing.

Dribbling into the path of an opponent.

Dribbling between two opponents when the space is not adequate.

Dribbling between an opponent and the boundary line, unless the space is such as to offer a reasonable chance for him to go through without contact.

Making contact with a dribbler whose head and shoulders have advanced in front of the defensive player. (If the dribbler passes an opponent without contact the greater responsibility for subsequent contact is on the opponent.)

Standing closer than a normal step behind a stationary opponent when screening.

Making contact with a stationary opponent when assuming a position alongside or in front of him.

Assuming a position so close to a moving opponent that he cannot avoid contact by stopping or changing direction.

Being in closer proximity while screening than one normal step from the opponent being screened. (The speed of the player to be screened will determine where the screener may take his stationary position.)

Moving, after assuming a screening position, in any direction except in the same direction and path as that of the opponent.

It is *not* a personal foul if a player's hand comes in contact with his opponent's hand while it is on the ball and is incidental to an attempt to play the ball.

Bonus Situation

PENALTY FOR A PERSONAL FOUL

The penalty for a personal foul is a free throw.

The Trail Official always *hands* the ball to the free thrower, whether it is the first or second free-throw.

TECHNICAL FOUL

A technical foul is a foul committed by a team or a nonplayer, or a player foul which does not involve contact with an opponent, or a player foul which involves unsportsmanlike contact with an opponent while the ball is dead.

A team, player, or nonplayer commits a technical foul by:

Delaying game by preventing the ball from being promptly made alive.

Allowing the game to develop into an actionless contest.

Being unready to start the game at either half.

Failing to supply scorers with names and numbers of each squad member who may participate. (Team foul.)

Failing to provide a list of the five starting players at least 3 minutes before starting time. (Team foul.)

Failing to be "reasonably active" on defense when the score is tied or the offender's team is behind and after a warning by an official.

Taking more than five time-outs in an untied game.

Having more than five squad members on the court at one time.

Failing to report a number change to the scorer or an official.

Participating after being disqualified.

Wearing an illegal number.

Grasping the basket.

Leaving the court for an unauthorized reason.

Using unsportsmanlike tactics.

Interfering with the ball after a goal.

Failing to pass the ball immediately to the nearest official after a goal.

Purposely delaying return to the court after being declared out of bounds.

Failing to raise hand at arm's length above head after being charged with a foul.

Using profanity.

Baiting an opponent or obstructing the vision of an opponent.

Climbing on a teammate to secure greater height to handle the ball.

Knowingly attempting a free throw to which he is not entitled.

Indicating resentment at being charged with a foul.

PENALTY FOR A TECHNICAL FOUL

The penalty for a technical foul is a free throw.

When the Trail Official administers a technical foul, no players are lined up on the free-throw lane.

After the free throw is completed following the technical foul, the ball is put in play again by giving it to the Lead Official waiting out-of-bounds at mid-court.

A team is allowed five team fouls per quarter (instead of six).

A player may be disqualified for any one flagrant foul.

OFFICIATING

The importance of good basketball officiating becomes more apparent with each season. Without competent officials, the game could not be played. Good officiating brings out the best playing ability of each player, while poor officiating can easily ruin a game. But good officials are not made overnight. They are the result of many years of study and practice gained through actual officiating. And that is why the IAABO was founded: to provide training assistance for the young official, and help the older official become more proficient through new techniques and planned programs. The IAABO provides tests, slides, and publications to enable those interested in officiating to learn the fundamentals in a series of steps toward the ultimate goal of becoming an official.

STEWART C. PAXTON
Executive Director,
International Association of
Approved Basketball Officials, Inc.

OFFICIALS

The officials should wear uniforms distinct from those of either team.

The officials should report on the playing court at least ten minutes before game time.

The Referee inspects and approves all equipment, including court, baskets, ball, backboards.

The Referee inspects timer's and scorer's signals.

The Referee designates the official timepiece and its operator.

The Referee designates the official scorebook and the official scorer.

The Referee is responsible for notifying each captain three minutes before each half is to begin.

The Referee checks and approves the score at the end of each half.

The Referee also:

1. Decides whether or not a goal shall count if officials disagree.
2. May forfeit the game when conditions warrant.
3. Decides upon matters on which the timers and scorers disagree.
4. Has the power to make decisions on any points not specifically covered by the rules.
5. Determines if ground rules are necessary.

Either official may penalize a player, coach, substitute, team attendant, or team follower for unsportsmanlike conduct.

Either official may call fouls on either team, or its supporters, if they act in such a way as to interfere with the proper conduct of the game. Discretion must be used by the officials.

Either official has the power to make decisions for infractions of the rules committed within or outside the boundary lines, and at any time from the beginning of play to the Referee's approval of the final score. This includes the periods when the game may be momentarily stopped for any reason.

The Referee's approval of the score book at the end of the game terminates the jurisdiction of the officials.

SCORERS AND TIMERS

The scorer(s) and timer(s) should report to the table in sufficient time (at least 20 minutes before game time) in order to secure line-ups and check the timing equipment so that all will be in readiness when officials arrive to give them pre-game instructions on ground rules.

A single timer and a single scorer may be used, provided they are trained men and acceptable to the Referee.

INSTRUCTIONS TO TIMEKEEPERS

ROUTINE

1. Consult Officials as to signals used to indicate a time-out and resumption of time.
2. Keep eyes on the officials throughout the game.
3. Check on the duration of time-outs, substitutions, time of periods, etc.
4. Note the position of ball when you signal end of any period or extra period. Timekeeper's signal ends these periods.
5. Check on duration of time between 1st and 2nd, 3rd and 4th periods, and between halves. Notify teams, Officials and Scorers the required number of minutes before the start of each half.
6. Seek designation from Referee as to which is Official Timepiece and its Operator.
7. It is strongly recommended that the operator of the official clock be an Adult.
8. When an electric clock is used, have a manual clock on hand in the event of failure of the electric clock.

START CLOCK

1. When ball is legally tapped on all jump balls.
2. When ball is touched in bounds, if resumption of play is by a throw-in after clock has been stopped. (Chopping motion.)
3. When ball is legally touched after a missed free throw and ball is to remain alive. (Chopping motion trail official.)

STOP CLOCK

1. When time expires at the end of a period.
2. When an official signals a foul.
3. When an official signals a jump ball.
4. When a violation occurs.
5. When an official orders time-out.
   a. To avoid unusual delay.
   b. To repair or adjustment equipment.
   c. For an injury or other emergency.
   d. Upon request of a player whose team has player control or when ball is dead.

GENERAL

If timekeeper's signal is not heard the timekeeper shall go on the court and notify the official—noting the position of the ball when time expires.

Referee shall appoint one timer as operator of the Timepiece.

The Official watch or clock shall be placed on the table between both timers. Another timepiece shall be used to check duration of time-outs.

LENGTH OF PERIODS

High School Games—8-minute quarters; 1 minute between quarters and extra periods and 10 minutes between halves; extra periods, 3 minutes.

College Games—Two 20-minute halves and 15 minutes between halves, 1 minute between extra periods; extra periods, 5 minutes.

All Games—Time-outs requested by players are for 1 minute. Time-outs to replace disqualified players are for 1 minute. Sound warning signal 15 seconds before end of time-out period. Time-outs for substitutions for injuries are for 1¼ minutes.

Timers are urged to study Rule 2, Section 12 and Rule 5 of the Official Rules Book.

INSTRUCTIONS TO SCORERS

1. Seek designation from Referee as to who is the official scorer and which is official scorebook and consult with him as to signals used to designate fouls and time-outs. The official scorer should wear a black and white striped garment.
2. Obtain names and numbers of all players who may participate in the game at least ten (10) minutes before the start of the game. At least three (3) minutes before scheduled starting time, have each team designate its five starting players. Report any failure to comply to referee.
3. Record field goals made, free throws made and missed, running summary of points scored, personal and technical fouls on each player, team personal fouls per half and time-outs.
4. Designate each goal and each foul thus:

Field goal	X or 2	Two shot foul	○○
Free throw attempt	○	Bonus opportunity	○○ or ○
Free throw made	⊕	Personal Foul	P1 P2 P3 P4 P5
Free throw violation	○ v	Technical Foul	T1 T2 T3 T4
Free throw substituted for original	○ s		

Field goals scored in wrong basket are not credited to any player but are credited to the team in a footnote. Points awarded for illegally touching ball or baskets are credited to the thrower. When a live ball goes in a basket, the last player who touched it causes it to go there.

5. *Notify official (a) when team has taken the legal five time-outs (b) when a player has had five personal fouls, (c) after a team has been charged with six personal fouls in either half of a game played in halves or four in a game played in quarters, (d) when a team has used time outs in excess of the five legal. In (b), (c) and (d) if play is in progress at time of discovery, withhold whistle until ball is dead or in control of offending team.*
6. Check with fellow scorer on each entry in score book, such as score, fouls, substitutions, charged time-outs, etc. If any discrepancy occurs notify referee at once on next dead ball—time out situation.
7. *Blow horn to stop game only when ball is dead and time is out.*
8. When a substitute reports (must be ready and entitled to enter game), signal when ball is dead and time is out and before change of status of ball is about to occur. Allow substitute to go on court only when Official beckons. Do not signal after ball has been placed at the disposal of a free thrower. If ball is dead after a free throw attempt, a substitution may be made. If thrower is to be replaced, be sure that it is legal for another player to attempt that particular throw. A substitute cannot replace a player designated to jump or designated to attempt a free throw, he must wait until the next dead ball, time-out, situation.

Score book of home team is the official book, unless referee rules otherwise. Scorers should be adults when possible and be equipped with a sounding device unlike that used by the Officials or Timers to signal the Officials.

Scorers should study Rule 2, Section 11 and Rules 3 and 5 of the Official Rules Book.

(Coaches are urged to paste these instructions in the front of their Score Book for future reference.)

FREE THROW VIOLATIONS: SIGNALS 2 AND 18
BASKET INTERFERENCE: USE SIGNALS 11 OR 12 AND 13

PROCEDURE IN CALLING A FOUL

PUTTING THE BALL IN PLAY
AFTER CALLING A FOUL

DOUBLE FOUL. The ball is put in play by a jump ball in the center circle.

MULTIPLE FOUL. The official places the ball at the disposal of the free thrower.

COMMON FOUL. Committed by a player while he, or a teammate, is in control of the ball. The official awards the ball to the opposing team at the out-of-bounds spot nearest the place where the foul was committed.

COMMON FOUL. Committed when the offending team has been charged during the half with six personal fouls in a game played in halves. The official follows the same procedure as in the multiple fouls situation but adds a bonus free throw following the permitted shot; the official gives the 1 and 1 signal.

When any foul, personal or technical, is called, the official:

Signals the fact with a sharp short whistle.

Signals for time out immediately.

Gives the sign indicating the nature of the foul.

Informs the player that he has committed a foul.

Informs the scorers verbally the number of the player committing the foul, and the number of free throws to be attempted.

Places the ball at the disposal of the free thrower.

Officials are expected to penalize the conduct of the coach and others on the bench if it is not in conformity with the rules. The coach is required to remain in the bench except for certain listed situations.

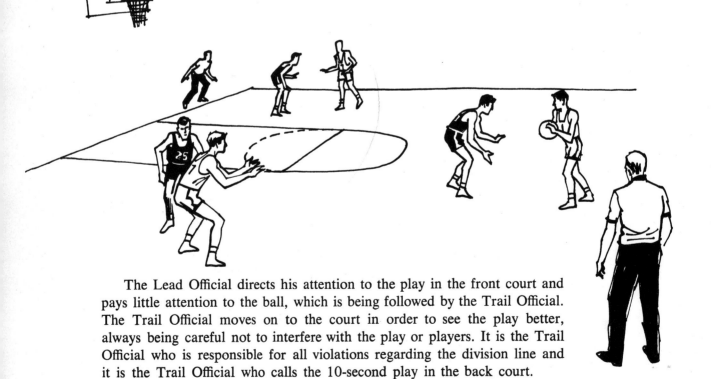

The Lead Official directs his attention to the play in the front court and pays little attention to the ball, which is being followed by the Trail Official. The Trail Official moves on to the court in order to see the play better, always being careful not to interfere with the play or players. It is the Trail Official who is responsible for all violations regarding the division line and it is the Trail Official who calls the 10-second play in the back court.

When a substitute enters the game, he may be beckoned in by either of the two officials. The official nearer the table usually signals the substitute to enter.

POSITION OF OFFICIALS
DURING TIME-OUT PERIOD

Official with the ball takes the position where play will be resumed. His fellow official stations himself just on the court near the scoring table with his back to the table, and is available when help is needed. He does not talk to the scorer or timer, and does not lean or sit on the table.

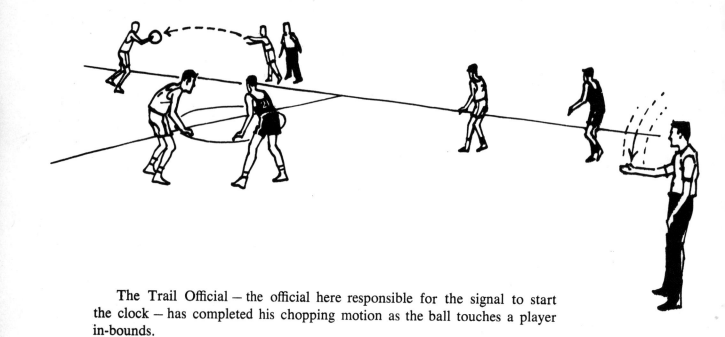

The Trail Official — the official here responsible for the signal to start the clock — has completed his chopping motion as the ball touches a player in-bounds.

The Lead Official hands (never tosses) the ball to the player out of bounds. The Lead Official will give the silent count of five seconds allowed for the throw-in. The Trail Official has his hand up, ready to bring it down in a chopping motion as soon as the ball touches a player on the court. The timer watches for this signal to start the clock.

the side line, the official shifts to the
situation near the side line. The Lead
der to follow the play from the best
view

The Trail Official moves to a position from which he can observe the
flight of the ball. He must be able to see if it passes over the top of the backboard, or if it strikes the supports. The Trail Official is responsible for the
action in the back half of the front court.

Both officials move with the action, taking up positions which give them
the clearest and most advantageous view.

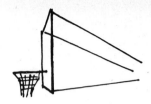

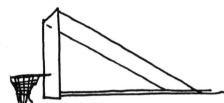

The Lead Official watches the front half of the front court. He is responsible for calling an infraction of the 3-second rule, as well as fouls and violations in this area. The Lead Official pays little attention to the flight of the ball as he is not looking above eye level.

When the ball goes out-of-bounds under the basket, the Lead Official hands the ball to the thrower-in on the nearer free-throw lane line extended. The ball is also taken to the nearer free-throw lane extended if the throw-in spot is behind the backboard.

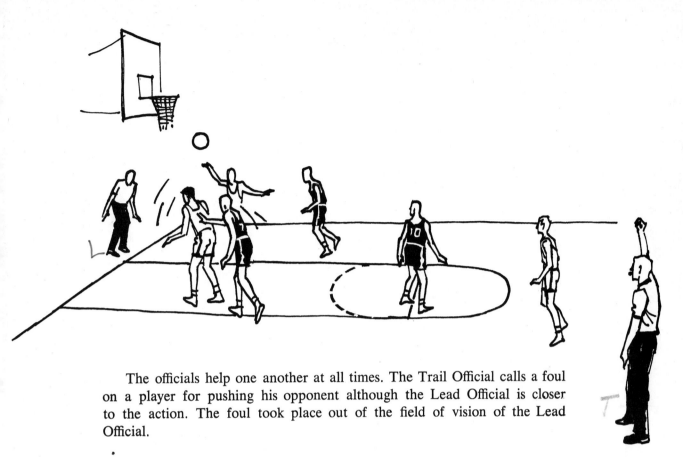

The officials help one another at all times. The Trail Official calls a foul on a player for pushing his opponent although the Lead Official is closer to the action. The foul took place out of the field of vision of the Lead Official.

After a goal has been awarded for basket interference or goal tending, the ball is given to the thrower-in to restart the game.

FLOOR PATTERNS

OFFENSE AND DEFENSE

by

BRUCE BASSETT

Athletic Director, International House

New York, N. Y.

OUT-OF-BOUNDS PLAY UNDER THE BASKET

X-1 screens for X-2 who cuts toward the basket, "picking off" the man guarding him, O-2, on the screen set by X-1.

If O-1, the man guarding X-1, switches defensive assignments with O-2 and picks up X-2 when he cuts off the screen set by X-1, the pass to X-2 in the preceding diagram will be ineffective. However, if O-1 switches, X-1 is left without a defensive man between him and the basket. If X-1 rolls off the screen he has set and cuts for the basket, he will be free for an easy shot.

OUT-OF-BOUNDS PLAY
FROM SIDELINES

X-2, the center, breaks upcourt and receives a pass from X-1, who is throwing in from out of bounds. X-3, the forward, has come up and set a screen on O, the man guarding X-1. After passing to X-2, X-1 cuts quickly toward the basket, picking off his defensive man on X-3's screen. X-2 gives X-1 a return pass and X-1 has a clear path to the basket. There are any number of possible out-of-bounds plays; most of them utilize a pass and a cut toward the basket.

BASIC FOOTWORK OF FORWARD PLAY

To receive a pass from the guard on his side of the floor, the forward should draw his defense man in toward the center of the floor and then break out toward the pass.

Pass

If the man guarding the forward overplays him by tending to play between the guard and the forward (in an attempt to prevent a pass from the guard to the forward) rather than between the forward and the basket, the forward can line his defense man up and then cut behind him for a pass and a clear path to the basket.

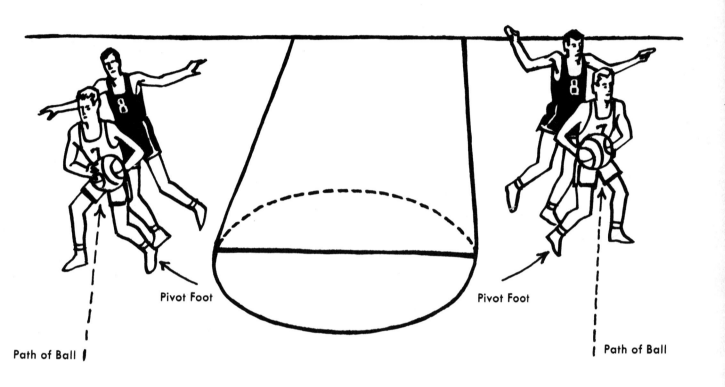

Path of Ball   Pivot Foot   Pivot Foot   Path of Ball

When the forward breaks up court and receives a pass from the guard he should use the foot nearest the middle of the court as his pivot foot.

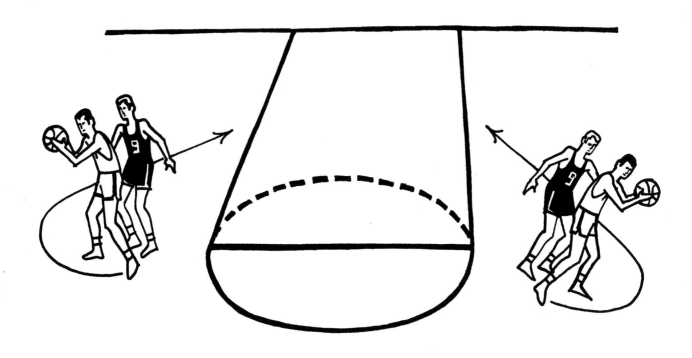

When the forward receives the pass from the guard, his back is toward the end line. Upon receiving the pass the forward has several options: If the defense man guarding the forward is not too close to him, the forward can shoot; if the defense man is playing the forward very tightly, the forward can pivot in the direction of the side line, pinning his defense man behind him, and drive toward the basket for a shot.

The pivot and drive toward the basket is made more effective if the forward is able to lure the defense man toward the center of the court and closer to him; then when the forward pivots in the direction of the side line and drives toward the basket, he will have the defensive man in a better position for pinning him behind the pivot. A pivot and feint toward the center of the court is conducive to putting the defensive man in this position.

The forward then pivots in the opposite direction.

This defensive man is pinned behind and a clear path to the basket is open.

ZONE DEFENSE

In a zone defense a team defends by assigning its men to be responsible for certain areas of the court rather than to certain men on the other team. Where a defensive man positions himself in the area depends upon where the ball is at the time. There are many types of zone defenses — that is, there are many ways that the court area around the basket being defended can be allocated. There are even defenses which combine a man-to-man defense with a zone defense.

Some of the basic zone defenses are:

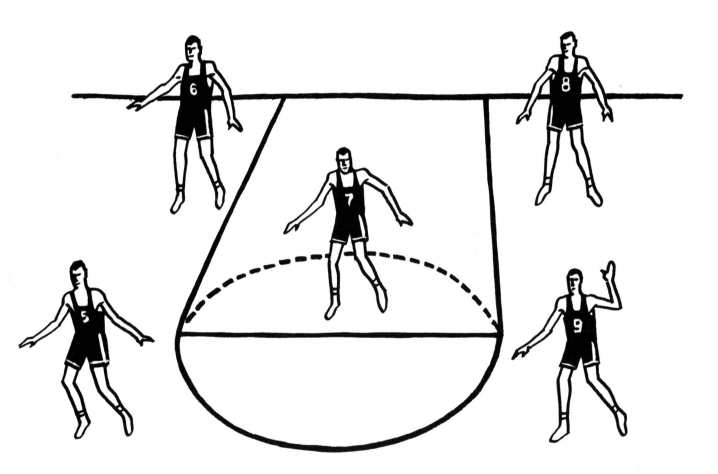

THE 2–1–2 ZONE

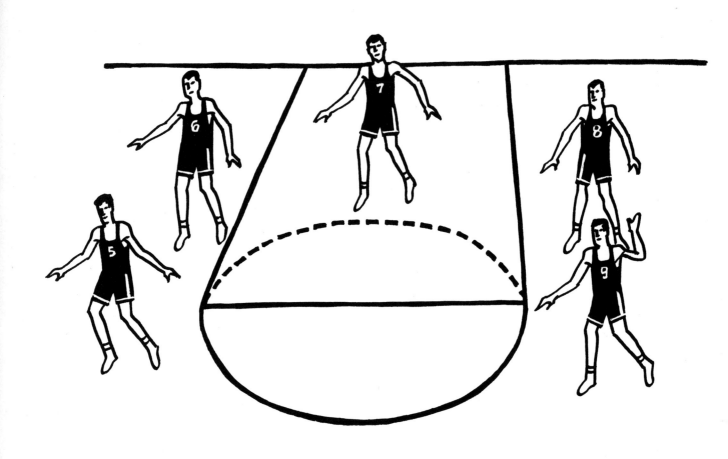

THE 1–2–2 ZONE

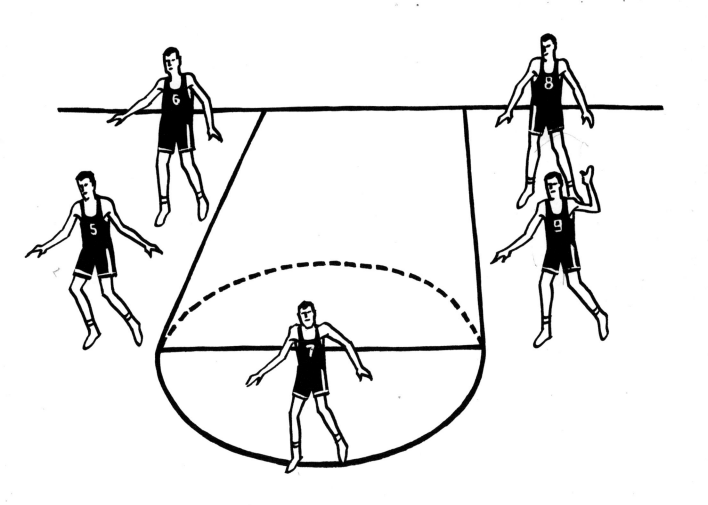

THE 2—2—1 ZONE

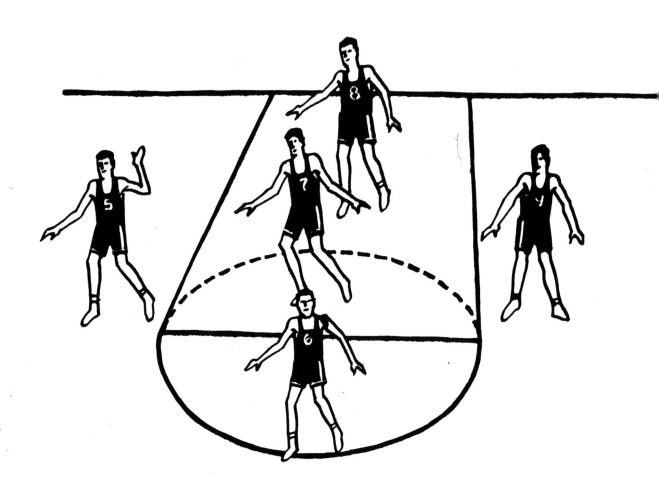

THE 1-3-1 ZONE

The area assigned to each of the players in a zone depends on the type of zone used and on the desires of the coach, which are influenced by such factors as height and speed of each player and the offensive abilities of the other team. Generally, the areas are assigned so that whenever the ball is on the periphery of the zone, there will be three defensive men in the line of the ball and the basket.

58

Taking the 2 - 1 - 2 zone as an example:

The shaded area is considered the end of the area in which the other team can pose an offensive threat and the area in which the zone defense can be effectively maintained. No player on the defensive team may go outside this area to defend. This limitation is set by the coach, just as is that of each of the sub-areas within the shaded area where each defensive player may move.

The offensive team usually attempts to break the zone defense by passing the ball quickly around the periphery until the defense has not shifted quickly enough to keep up with the ball and a free shot is open.

ZONE SHIFT

Example of how a 2 - 1 - 2 zone might shift with the movement of the ball.

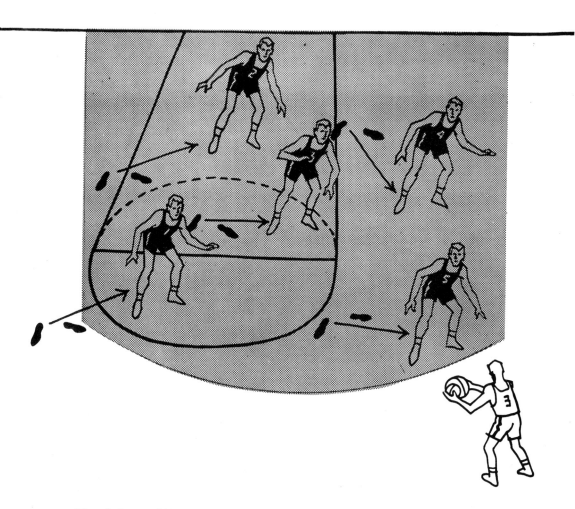

The defense shifts as the ball is moved around the periphery of the zone and tries to keep the zone impenetrable. This forces the offensive team to shoot from outside the zone where the accuracy is generally less and gives the defensive team playing the zone more men grouped near the basket to gather the rebounds from missed shots.

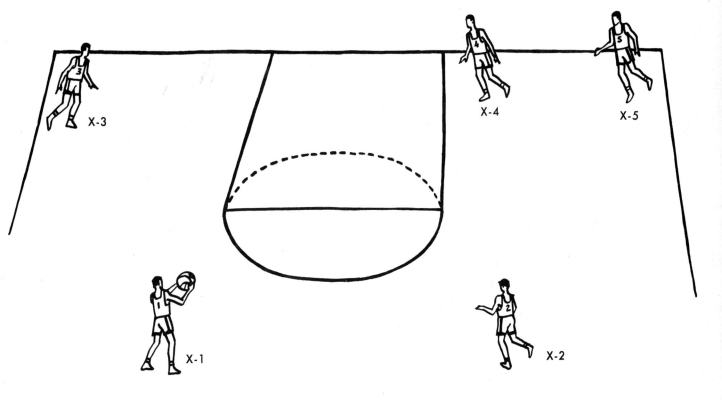

SAMPLE OFFENSIVE PLAY AGAINST
MAN-TO-MAN DEFENSE

The guard with the ball, in this case X-1, drives into the middle until
he is effectively checked by his defensive man or until he reaches the free
throw line.

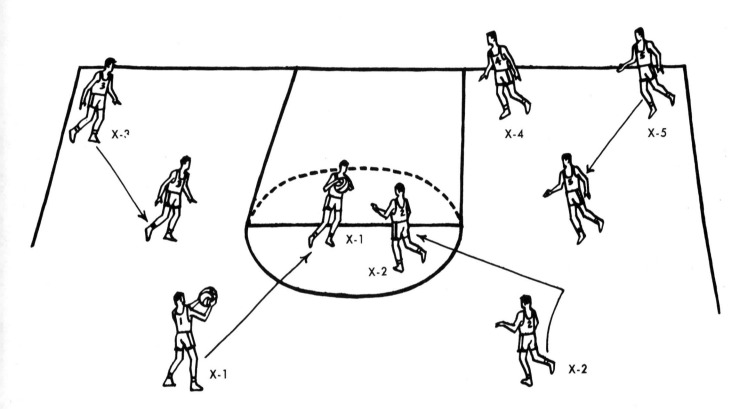

Then X-1 turns his back to the basket and looks for X-2, who has faked as if to cut toward the corner and has timed his cut to coincide with X-1's turn toward him. At this point there are several options:

If X-1 passes the ball to X-2, X-2 may take a set shot if his defensive man, O-2, has dropped behind X-1. However, if either O-1 or O-2 attempts to get around X-1 to guard X-2, X-2 can drive on the other side of X-1. X-1 can also roll toward the basket and the defense will be left with one defensive man trying to guard two offensive men. If the remaining defensive man, O-1, picks up X-2 as he drives toward the basket, X-1 is open for a pass and an easy shot; if O-1 does not pick up X-2, X-2 has a clear path to the basket.

If a defensive man comes out to guard X-2 from the other side of X-1, then the situation is just reversed, and X-2 drives to his right past X-1.

O-1 must decide whether to guard X-1 or X-2; whichever one he guards, the other is left free. O-2 is screened by X-1 when he tries to follow X-2's drive; both X-1 and X-2 are ahead of him.

As another alternative, X-1 can maintain his dribble when he turns after dribbling into the middle, let X-2 cut by him, and then drive off of X-2. This usually gives X-1 clearance for a short shot, but care must be taken that the violation of a moving screen is not committed. Basically, these are the alternatives from which the two guards can choose their play. Of course, the effectiveness of these maneuvers can be heightened by some added feints and options. When the guards X-1 and X-2 become more familiar with their options, their moves will be aimed primarily at taking advantage of what the defense does.

For example, if O-2 guarding X-2 anticipates the pass from X-1 to X-2, then X-2 can fake a cut behind X-1 and then cut straight for the basket and the pass from X-1. Note how O-2 overplays X-2 in anticipation of a cut behind X-1.

Assuming that X-1 and X-2 do not use their options, the pattern continues, bringing into play the forwards who have broken out of the corners. X-2 upon receiving the pass from X-1 has an option of passing either to X-3 or X-5.

Assuming X-2 passes to X-5, the opposite forward, X-3, should come out further for defensive purposes. The offensive team must always have men back far enough to provide a defense if the defensive team should suddenly obtain the ball.

Upon passing the ball to X-5, X-2 cuts toward the basket and X-5 has several options. He may shoot if he is open, he may pass back to X-2 who is cutting toward the basket, he may drive toward the basket, or he may drive toward the center of the floor. Whatever happens, X-1 must drop back for defensive purposes as soon as X-2 has cut by him.

If X-5 does not exercise another option he drives across the court.

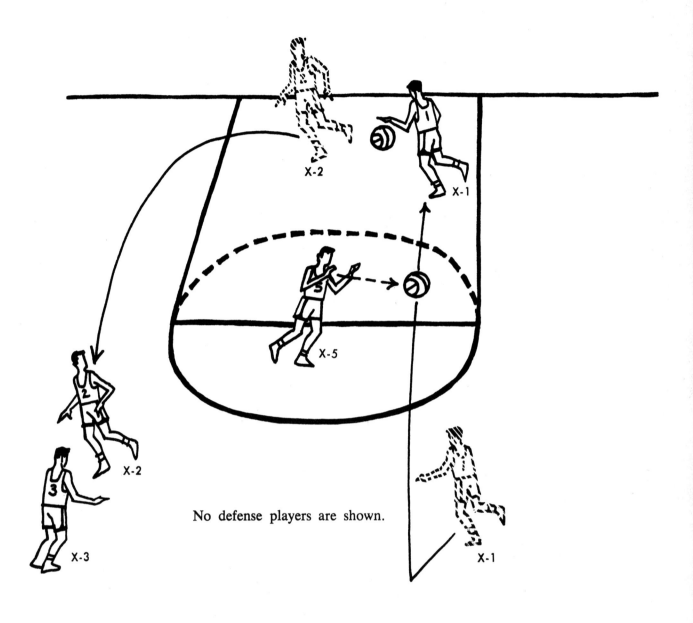

No defense players are shown.

In driving across the court, X-5 may find freedom to shoot. If not, he can stop and turn his back to the basket in approximately the same position as X-1 did at the beginning of the pattern. Meanwhile, X-1 has drifted out toward the center as if solely for defensive purposes should there be a sudden turnover of the ball to the defensive team. In fact, both O-3 and O-1 will be lulled into thinking that their men, X-3 and X-1 are out of the play and as a consequence they will relax. When X-5 turns in his dribble across the court, X-1 who has been drifting out should suddenly turn and cut toward the basket. O-1 will probably be left behind by X-1's sudden reversal. X-2, who has cut to the basket, must continue moving and come back out, both to free the middle of the court and also for defensive purposes.

Note that X-1 and X-5 have options similar to the ones X-1 and X-2 had when they crossed at the beginning of the pattern. However, these would only be utilized if O-1 is not left behind by X-1's sudden reversal and cut toward the basket. Of course, upon passing off to X-1, X-5 should also roll toward the basket, leaving O-1 behind him and making O-5 choose between guarding X-1 or X-5.

If O-1 is not left behind, X-1 will cut by X-5 so as to run O-1 into the screen of X-5.

If O-3 turns his head from X-3 or relaxes his because the play is occurring behind him, X-3 can cut for the basket and receive a pass from X-5.

Whenever X-1 or X-2, the guards, cut through to the basket, they must come right back out so as to keep the middle open and to be ready to change to defense if the other team gets the ball and starts toward its basket.

Throughout this sequence of options, the center, X-4, must roam along the back line so as to keep himself and his defensive man O-4 out of the way and yet be available for a pass and in good position to take a rebound after any shot. Where this position is depends on many factors of varying importance. Some of these factors are where the ball is, what options are likely to be used, where the rest of the team is positioned, and where the man guarding him is.

BASKETBALL RULES

Official Rules printed by special permission of the National Collegiate Athletic Association.

RULE 4 — DEFINITIONS

BASKET SECTION 1. A *Basket* is the 18-inch ring, its flanges and braces and appended net through which players attempt to throw the ball. A team's own basket is the one into which its players try to throw the ball. The visiting team shall have the irrevocable choice of baskets at which it may practice before the game and this basket shall be its choice for the 1st half. The teams shall change baskets for the 2nd half.

BLOCKING SECTION 2. *Blocking* is personal contact which impedes the progress of an opponent who does not have the ball.

CHANGE OF STATUS SECTION 3. *Change of status* is the time at which a dead ball becomes alive or a live ball becomes dead. Change of status is about to occur when:

(a) A player has started to make a throw-in; or
(b) 80% of the time limit count has expired; or
(c) An Official is ready to make the toss for a jump; or
(d) An Official starts to place the ball at the disposal of a free thrower.

IN CONTROL — PLAYER, TEAM SECTION 4. *A player is in control* when he is holding a live ball or dribbling it. *A team is in control* when a player of the team is in control and also while a live ball is being passed between teammates. Team control continues until: there is a try for goal; or an opponent secures control; or the ball becomes dead. There is no team control: during a jump ball; a throw-in; a try for goal; or during the tapping of a rebound. In these situations, team control is reestablished when a player secures control.

DISQUALIFIED PLAYER SECTION 5. *A Disqualified Player* is one who is barred from further participation in the game because of committing his fifth personal foul, or a flagrant foul, or for infraction of Rule 10-4a or b.

DRIBBLE SECTION 6. *A Dribble* is ball movement caused by a player in control who throws or taps the ball in the air or onto the floor and then touches it once or several times or catches it. *The dribble ends* when the dribbler: (a) touches the ball with both hands simultaneously; or (b) permits it to come to rest while he is in contact with it; or (c) loses control of it (4-3).

An Air-Dribble is that part of a dribble during which the dribbler throws or taps the ball in the air and then touches it before it touches the floor.

QUESTION (1) — Is a player dribbling while tapping the ball during a jump, or when a pass rebounds from his hand, or when he fumbles, or when he taps a rebound or a pass away from other players who are attempting to get it? ANSWER — No. The player is not in control under these conditions.

QUESTION (2) — Is it a dribble when a player stands still and: (a) bounces the ball; or (b) holds the ball and touches it to the floor once or more? ANSWER — (a) Yes, (b) No.

EXTRA PERIOD SECTION 7. *Extra Period* is the extension of playing time necessary to break a tie score.

FOUL SECTION 8. (a) *A Foul* is an infraction of the rules, the penalty for which is one or more free throws unless it is a double foul, or is a player control foul in which case the free throw provision is canceled. For convenience, a personal foul, which is neither flagrant nor intentional nor committed against a player trying for field goal, nor a part of a double or multiple foul, is termed a common foul.

DOUBLE FOUL (b) *A Double Foul* is a situation in which two opponents commit personal fouls against each other at approximately the same time. *A False Double Foul* is a situation in which there are fouls by both teams, the second of which occurs before the clock is started following the first, but such that at least one of the attributes of a double foul is absent.

MULTIPLE FOUL (c) *A Multiple Foul* is a situation in which two or more teammates commit personal fouls against the same opponent at approximately the same time. *A False Multiple Foul* is a situation in which there are two or more fouls by the same team and such that the last foul is committed before the clock is started following the first, and such that at least one of the attributes of a multiple foul is absent.

PERSONAL FOUL (d) *A Personal Foul* (10-8) is a player foul which involves contact with an opponent while the ball is alive or after the ball is in possession of a player for a throw-in.

PLAYER CONTROL FOUL (e) *A Player Control Foul* is a common foul committed by a player while he or a teammate is in control.

TECHNICAL FOUL (f) *A Technical Foul* (10-1 to 7) is a foul by a nonplayer or a player foul which does not involve contact with an opponent, or a player foul which involves unsportsmanlike contact with an opponent while the ball is dead, except as indicated in last clause of (d) above.

FREE THROW SECTION 9. *A Free Throw* is the privilege given a player to score one point by an unhindered try for goal from within the free throw circle and behind the free throw line. A free throw starts when the ball is given to the free thrower at the free throw line or is placed on the line. It ends when: the try is successful; or it is certain the try will not be successful; or when the try touches the floor or any player; or when the ball becomes dead.

FRONT AND BACK COURT SECTION 10. (a) *A Team's Front Court* consists of that part of the court between its end line and the nearer edge of the division line and including its basket and the inbounds part of its backboard. *A Team's Back Court* consists of the rest of the court including its opponent's basket and inbounds part of the backboard and the entire division line.

(b) *A live ball is in the front or back court* of the team in control as follows:

(1) A ball which is in contact with a player or with the court is in the back court if either the ball or the player (either player if the ball is touching more than one) is touching the back court. It is in the front court if neither the ball nor the player is touching the back court.

(2) A ball which is not in contact with a player or the court retains the same status as when it was last in contact with a player or the court.

QUESTION – From the front court, A passes the ball across the division line. It touches a teammate who is in the air after leaping from the back court or it touches an Official in the back court. Is the ball in the back court? ANSWER – Yes. See 4-15.

HELD BALL SECTION 11. *Held Ball* occurs when:

(a) Opponents have hands so firmly on the ball that control cannot be obtained without undue roughness; or

(b) A closely guarded player anywhere in his front court holds the ball for 5 seconds; or

(c) A team, in its front court, controls the ball for 5 seconds in an area enclosed by screening teammates; or

(d) In an attempt to consume time, a closely guarded player within a few feet of a front court boundary intersection dribbles, or combines dribbling and holding the ball for 5 seconds; or

(e) In an attempt to consume time, a closely guarded player, in his mid-court area, dribbles, or combines dribling and holding the ball for 5 seconds.

The player in control is closely guarded when his opponent is in a guarding stance at a distance not exceeding 6 feet from him.

QUESTION – Is it a held ball merely because the player holding the ball is lying or sitting on the floor? ANSWER – No.

HOLDING SECTION 12. *Holding* is personal contact with an opponent which interferes with his freedom of movement.

NOTE – *"Guarding from the rear" which results in personal contact is a personal foul. Officials should give special attention to this type of infraction. The mere fact that the defensive player is attempting to play the ball does not justify him in making contact with the player in control. A held ball decision is not warranted merely on the grounds the defensive player gets his hand on the ball. Usually such a decision is unfair to the player who has control. If the defensive player causes contact in an attempt to get at the ball from an unfavorable position he should be penalized.*

JUMP BALL SECTION 13. *A Jump Ball* is a method of putting the ball into play by tossing it up between two opponents in one of the three circles. It begins when the ball leaves the Official's hand and ends as outlined in Rule 6-4.

LACK OF ACTION SECTION 14. *Lack of Sufficient Action* is the failure of the responsible team to force play as required by the Comments on the Rules.

LOCATION OF A PLAYER SECTION 15. *The Location of a Player* (or non-player) is determined by where he is touching the floor as far as being inbounds or out of bounds or being in the front court or back court is concerned. When he is in the air from a leap, his status with reference to these two factors is the same as at the time he was last in contact with the floor or an extension of the floor such as a bleacher. When the ball touches an Official, it is the same as touching the floor at the Official's location.

MID-COURT AREA SECTION 16. *The Mid-Court Area* of a team is that part of its front court between the division line and a parallel imaginary line approximately 3 feet outside that part of the free throw circle which is farthest from the end line.

MULTIPLE THROW SECTION 17. *A Multiple Throw* is a succession of free throws attempted by the same team.

PASS SECTION 18. *A Pass* is movement of the ball caused by a player, who throws, bats or rolls the ball to another player.

PENALTY SECTION 19. *A Penalty* for a foul is the charging of the offender with the foul and awarding one or more free throws, or awarding the ball to the opponents for a throw-in. The penalty for a violation is the awarding of the ball to the opponents for a throw-in or one or more points or a substitute free throw.

PIVOT Section 20. *A Pivot* takes place when a player who is holding the ball steps once or more than once in any direction with the same foot, the other foot, called the pivot foot, being kept at its point of contact with the floor.

RULE Section 21. *A Rule* is one of the groups of laws which governs the game. A game law (commonly called a rule) sometimes states or implies that the ball is dead or that a foul or violation is involved. If it does not, it is assumed the ball is alive and no foul or violation has occurred to affect the given situation. A single infraction is not complicated by a second infraction unless so stated or implied.

TRAVELING Section 22. *Running with the Ball* (traveling) is moving a foot or the feet in any direction in excess of prescribed limits while holding the ball. The limits follow:

Item 1. A player who receives the ball while standing still may pivot, using either foot as the pivot foot.

Item 2. A player, who receives the ball while his feet are moving or who is dribbling, may stop as follows:

(a) If he catches the ball while *both feet* are off the floor and:

(1) *He alights with both feet* touching the floor simultaneously, he may pivot using either foot as the pivot foot; or

(2) *He alights with first one foot* touching the floor followed by the other, he may pivot using the first foot to touch the floor as the pivot foot; or

(3) *He alights on one foot,* he may jump off that foot and alight with both feet simultaneously, but he may not pivot before releasing the ball.

(b) If he catches the ball while only *one foot* is off the floor:

(1) *He may step* with the foot which is off the floor and may then pivot using the other foot as the pivot foot; or

(2) *He may jump* with the foot which is on the floor and alight with both feet simultaneously, but he may not pivot before releasing the ball.

Item 3. After a player has come to a stop, he may pass or throw for goal under the following conditions:

(a) In Items 1, 2a(1), 2a(2) and 2b(1), he may lift either foot, but if he lifts his pivot foot or jumps before he passes or throws for goal, the ball must leave his hand before the pivot foot again touches the floor; or if he has jumped before either foot touches the floor.

(b) In Items 2a(3) and 2b(2), he may lift either foot or jump before he passes or throws for goal. However, the ball must leave his hand before a foot which has left the floor retouches it.

Item 4. A player who receives the ball as in Item 1 or a player, who comes to a stop after he receives the ball while he is moving his feet, may start a dribble under the following conditions:

(a) In Items 1, 2a(1), 2a(2) and 2b(1), the ball must leave his hand before the pivot foot leaves the floor.

(b) In Items 2a(3) and 2b(2), the ball must leave his hand before either foot leaves the floor.

QUESTION (1) — Is it traveling if a player falls to the floor while holding the ball? ANSWER — No, unless he makes progress by sliding.

QUESTION (2) — A^1 jumps to throw the ball. B^1 prevents the throw by placing one or both hands firmly on the ball so that: (a) A^1; or (b) A^1 and B^1 both return to the floor holding it. ANSWER — Held ball. However, if A^1 voluntarily drops the ball before he returns to the floor and he then touches the ball before it is touched by another player, A^1 has committed a traveling violation.

SCREEN Section 23. *A Screen* is legal action of a player who, without causing contact, delays or prevents an opponent from reaching a desired position.

THROW-IN Section 24. *A Throw-in* is a method of putting the ball in play from out of bounds in accordance with Rule 7. The throw-in begins when the ball is at the disposal of the player or team entitled to it and ends when the passed ball touches or is touched by an inbounds player other than thrower-in.

TRY FOR FIELD GOAL Section 25. *A try for field goal* is an attempt by a player to score 2 points by throwing the ball into his basket. The try starts when the player begins the motion which habitually precedes actual throw. The try ends when the throw is successful; or it is certain the throw will not be successful; or when the throw ball touches the floor or any player; or when the ball becomes dead. The *thrower* continues to be a thrower until the ball is clearly in flight.

VIOLATION Section 26. *A Violation* is a rule infraction of the type listed in Rule 9.

RULE 8 — FREE THROW

POSITIONS DURING ATTEMPT Section 1. *When a free throw is awarded,* an official shall take the ball to the free throw line of the offended team. After allowing reasonable time for players to take their positions, he shall put the ball in play by placing it at the disposal of the free thrower. The same procedure shall be followed for each free throw of a multiple throw. During a free throw for personal foul, each of the lane spaces adjacent to the end line shall be occupied by one opponent of the free thrower. A teammate of the free thrower is entitled to the next adjacent lane space on each side and to each other alternate position along each lane line. Not more than one player may occupy any part of the first, second, or third lane spaces. If the ball is to become dead when the last free throw for a specific penalty is not successful, players shall not take positions along the free throw lane.

NOTE—To avoid disconcerting the free-thrower, neither Official should stand in the free throw lane or the lane extended.

WHO ATTEMPTS SECTION 2. The free throw or throws awarded because of a personal foul shall be attempted by the offended player. If such player must withdraw because of injury or disqualification, his substitute shall attempt the throw or throws unless no substitute is available, in which event any teammate may attempt the throw or throws.

NOTE — See Question (1) under Rule 2-11.

SECTION 3. The free throw awarded because of a technical foul may be attempted by any player, including an entering substitute, of the offended team.

10-SECOND LIMIT SECTION 4. *The try for goal shall be made within 10 seconds after the ball has been placed*

at the disposal of the free thrower at the free throw line. This shall apply to each free throw.

NEXT PLAY SECTION 5. *After a free throw* which is not followed by another free throw, the ball shall be put in play by a throw-in: (a) as after a field goal (7-5) if the try is for a personal foul and is successful; or (b) by any player of the free-thrower's team from out of bounds at mid-court if the free throw is for a technical foul.

BALL IN PLAY IF GOAL IS MISSED SECTION 6. *If a free throw for a personal foul is unsuccessful,* or if there is a multiple throw for a personal foul (or fouls) and the last free throw is unsuccessful, the ball remains alive.

If there is a multiple throw and both a personal and technical foul are involved, the tries shall be attempted in the order in which the related fouls were called and if the last try is for a technical foul the ball shall be put in play as after any technical foul.

CENTER BALL AFTER FALSE DOUBLE FOUL SECTION 7. After the last free throw following a false double foul (4-7b), the ball shall be put in play by a jump at center between any two opponents.

QUESTION—Two free throws are awarded to A and before time is in, one free throw is awarded to B. What is the correct procedure? ANSWER — Jump ball at center after the third free throw.

RULE 9 — VIOLATIONS AND PENALTIES

A PLAYER SHALL NOT — FREE THROW SECTION 1. *Violate the free throw provisions:* (a) The try shall be attempted from within the free throw circle and behind the free throw line. (b) After the ball is placed at the disposal of a free thrower (1) he shall throw within 10 seconds and in such a way that the ball enters the basket or touches the ring before the free throw ends; (2) no opponent may disconcert the free thrower; and (3) the thrower shall not have either foot beyond the vertical plane of that edge of the free throw line which is farther from the basket; and no other player of either team shall have either foot beyond the vertical plane or cylinder of the outside edge of any lane boundary, nor beyond the vertical plane of any edge of the space (2 inches by 36 inches) designated by a lane space mark or the space (12 inches by 36 inches) designated by a neutral zone mark, nor enter nor leave the lane space which is nearest the end line. The restrictions in (3)

apply until the ball touches the ring or backboard or until the free throw ends. (c) An opponent of the free thrower shall occupy each lane space adjacent to the end line during the try.

PENALTY — (1) If violation is by the free thrower or his teammate only, no point can be scored by that throw. Ball becomes dead when violation occurs. Ball is awarded out of bounds on the sideline to the free thrower's team opposite enter circle after a technical foul, and to any opponent out of bounds at either end of the free throw line extended after a personal foul. (2) If violation is by the free thrower's opponent only: if the try is successful, the goal counts and violation is disregarded; if it is not successful, a substitute throw shall be attempted by the same thrower under conditions the same as for the throw for which it is substituted. In these cases, ball becomes dead when the free throw ends. (3) If there is a violation by each team, ball becomes dead when violation by the free thrower's team occurs, no point can be scored, and play shall be resumed by a jump between any two opponents in the nearest circle. The out of bounds provision in penalty item (1) and the jump ball provision in penalty item (3) do not apply if the free throw is to be followed by another free throw, or if there are free throws by both teams. In penalty item (3), if an opponent of the thrower touches the free throw before it has touched the ring, the violation for the failure to touch the ring is ignored.

> QUESTION – During a free throw by A^1, B^1 pushes A^2 and also B^1 or B^2 is in the lane too soon. ANSWER – If the free throw is not successful, award a substitute free throw and also penalize the foul.

SECTION 2. *Cause the ball to go out of bounds.*

> QUESTION – Dribbler in control steps on or outside a boundary, but does not touch the ball while he is out of bounds. Is this a violation? ANSWER – Yes.

THROW-IN SECTION 3. *Violate provisions governing the throw-in.* The thrower-in shall not: (a) leave the designated throw-in spot; (b) fail to pass the ball directly into the court so that after it crosses the boundary line it touches or is touched by another player on the court before going out of bounds; (c) consume more than 5 seconds from the time the throw-in starts until it touches or is touched by a player on the court; (d) carry the ball onto the court; (e) touch it in the court before it has touched another player; nor (f) throw the ball so that it enters a basket before touching anyone.

No player shall (g) have any part of his person over the boundary line before the ball has been passed across the line; nor (h) becomes the thrower-in after an Official has designated another player.

> QUESTION – On throw-in, A steps on the line or reaches through its plane while holding ball. ANSWER – Violation. Allowance should be made if space is limited.

SECTION 4. *Run with the ball, kick it, strike it with the fist* or cause it to enter and pass through the basket from below.

NOTE – Kicking the ball is a violation only when it is a positive act; accidentally striking the ball with the foot or leg is not a violation.

> QUESTION – What is kicking the ball? ANSWER – Kicking the ball is striking it intentionally with the knee or any part of the leg or foot below the knee. It is a fundamental of basketball that the ball must be played with the hands.

DOUBLE DRIBBLE SECTION 5. *Dribble a second time* after his first dribble has ended, unless it is after he has lost control because of: (a) a try for field goal; or (b) a bat by an opponent; or (c) a pass or fumble which has then touched another player. He shall not make more than one air-dribble during a dribble.

JUMP BALL SECTION 6. *Violate any provision of 6-4.* If both teams simultaneously commit violations during the jump ball, or if the Official makes a bad toss, the toss should be repeated.

3-SECOND RULE SECTION 7. *Remain for more than 3 seconds* in that part of his free throw lane between the end line and the farther edge of the free throw line while the ball is in control of his team. Allowance shall be made for a player who, having been in the restricted area for less than 3 seconds, dribbles in to try for goal.

> QUESTION – Does the 3-second restriction apply: (a) to a player who has only one foot touching the lane boundary; or (b) while the ball is dead or in flight on a try? ANSWER – (a) Yes, the line is part of the lane. (b) No, the team is not in control.

10-SECOND RULE SECTION 8. *Be* (and his team shall not be) *in continuous control* of a ball which is in his back court for more than 10 consecutive seconds.

BALL IN BACK COURT SECTION 9. *Be the first to touch* a ball which he or a teammate caused to go from front court to back court by being the last to touch the ball while it was in control of his team and before it went to the back court.

Exception: This restriction does not apply if, after a jump ball in the center circle, the player who first secures control of the tapped ball is in his front court at the time he secures such control and he causes the ball to go to his back court not later than the first loss of player control by him and provided it is the first time the ball is in his back court following the jump ball.

> QUESTION – A receives pass in his front court and throws ball to his back court where ball: (a) is touched by a teammate; or (b) goes directly out of bounds; or (c) lies or bounces with all players hesitating to touch it. ANSWER – Violation when touched in (a). In (b) it is a violation for going out of bounds. In (c) ball is alive so that B may secure control. If A touches ball first, it is a violation. The ball continues to be in team control of A and if A does not touch it the ten-second count starts when ball arrives in the back court.

SECTION 10. Excessively swing his arms or elbows, even though there is no contact with an opponent. (See Comments.)

PENALTY — (Sections 2 to 10.) Ball becomes dead or remains dead when violation occurs. Ball is awarded to a nearby opponent for a throw-in at the out of bounds, spot nearest the violation. If the ball passes through a basket during the dead ball period immediately following a violation, no point can be scored and the ball is awarded to an opponent out of bounds at either end of that free throw line extended nearer the goal through which the ball was thrown.

BASKET INTERFERENCE AND GOAL TENDING   Section
11. (a) *Touch the ball or basket* when the ball is on or within either basket; nor touch the ball when it: (b) is touching the cylinder having the ring as its lower base; or (c) is not touching the cylinder but is in downward flight during a try for field goal while the entire ball is above the basket ring level and before the ball has touched the ring or the try has ended.

Exception: In (a) or (b), if a player near his own basket has his hand legally in contact with the ball, it is not a violation if his contact with the ball continues after it enters the cylinder, or if, in such action, he touches the basket.

PENALTY — If violation is at the opponent's basket, offended team is awarded one point if during a free throw and two points in any other case. The crediting of the score and subsequent procedure is the same as if the awarded score had resulted from the ball having gone through the basket except that the Official shall hand the ball to a player of the team entitled to the throw-in.

If violation is at a team's own basket, no points can be scored and the ball is awarded to the offended team at the out of bounds spot on the side at either end of the free throw line extended.

If there is a violation by both teams, play shall be resumed by a jump ball between any two opponents in the nearest circle.

QUESTION — While the ball is in flight on a try for field goal by A, a teammate of A pushes an opponent. After this personal foul, the ball is on the ring when B bats it away. Which infraction should be penalized? AN-SWER — Both. Award 2 points to A. Then penalize for personal foul.

NEMADJI SCHOOL
Hwy. 35
Superior, Wisconsin

I.M.C.